States

WASHINGTON

WITHDRAWN

by Bridget Parker

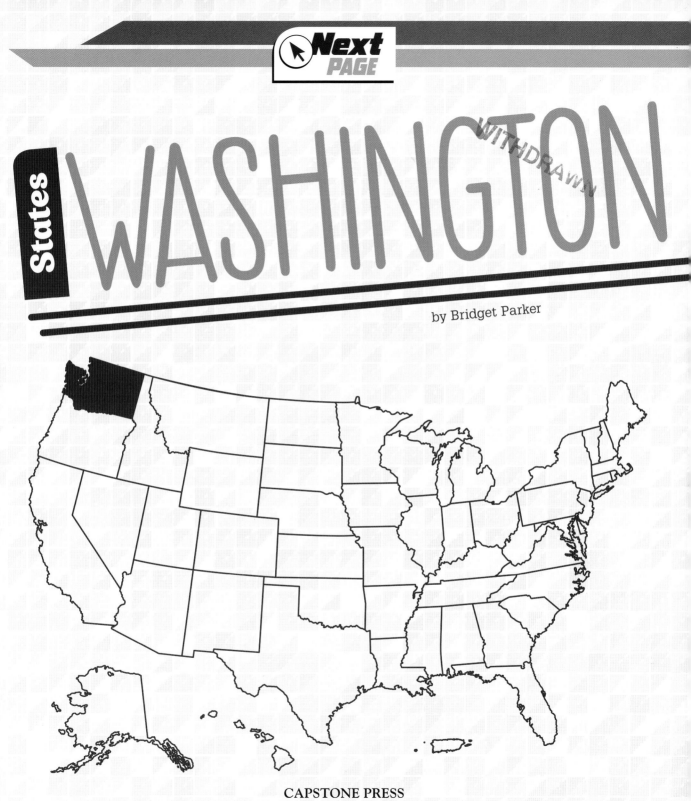

CAPSTONE PRESS
a capstone imprint

Next Page Books are published by Capstone Press,
1710 Roe Crest Drive, North Mankato, Minnesota 56003
www.mycapstone.com

Library of Congress Cataloging-in-Publication Data
Cataloging-in-publication information is on file with the Library of
Congress.
ISBN 978-1-5157-0435-5 (library binding)
ISBN 978-1-5157-0494-2 (paperback)
ISBN 978-1-5157-0546-8 (ebook PDF)

Editorial Credits
Jaclyn Jaycox, editor; Ashlee Suker, designer; Morgan Walters,
media researcher; Tori Abraham, production specialist

Photo Credits
Capstone Press: Angi Gahler, map 4, 7; CriaImages.com: Jay
Robert Nash Collection, top 18; Dreamstime: Jerry Coli, bottom 19,
Martynelson, 27; Library of Congress: Boyd and Braas, middle 18;
Newscom: akg-images, 12, BEN NELMS, 29, ZUMAPRESS/Brian
Cahn, bottom left 21; One Mile Up, Inc., flag, seal 23; Shutterstock:
1tomm, 11, 2009fotofriends, 5, Action Sports Photography, top 19,
Al Mueller, bottom left 20, alens, bottom 24, Becky Sheridan, bottom
right 21, Candace Hartley, top right 21, Denise Lett, 17, Edmund
Lowe Photography, 7, Eugene Kalenkovich, 6, Featureflash, middle
19, Galyna Andrushko, 10, Jonathan Lingel, 28, JStone, bottom 18,
karamysh, bottom left 8, 15, Lonnie Gorsline, 9, bottom right 20,
M. Bailey, top 24, Mike Peters, cover, Monika Wieland, top left 21,
SEASTOCK Video, bottom right 8, steve estvanik, 16, tab62, top right
20, teekaygee, middle left 21, tobkatrina, 14, Zack Frank, 13; United
States Department of Agriculture: Loren St. John, middle right 21;
Wikimedia: Brown, William Compton, 26, Ebustad, top left 20, www.
cmhg.gc.ca, 25

All design elements by Shutterstock

Printed and bound in China.
0316/CA21600187
012016   009436F16

TABLE OF CONTENTS

Want to take your research further? Ask your librarian if your school subscribes to PebbleGo Next. If so, when you see this helpful symbol (↖) throughout the book, log onto www.pebblegonext.com for bonus downloads and information.

LOCATION

Washington lies on the Pacific Coast in the northwestern part of the country. Only two U.S. states border Washington. Idaho lies to its east. Oregon is to the south. Washington lies to the south of British Columbia, Canada. The Pacific Ocean forms the state's western border. Washington's capital is Olympia. The state's three largest cities are Seattle, Spokane, and Tacoma.

PebbleGo Next Bonus! To print and label your own map, go to www.pebblegonext.com and search keywords:

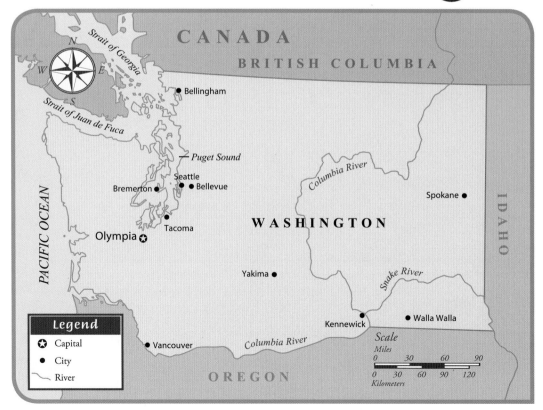

The Pacific Coast stretches out along Washington's western border.

GEOGRAPHY

Washington is famous for its natural beauty. It has snow-covered mountains, rolling hills, evergreen forests, and beautiful coastal waters. The Olympic Mountains and Puget Sound lie near the Pacific Ocean. Puget Sound is a long, narrow ocean bay with more than 300 islands. The Cascade Range divides the state in half. Mount Rainier, the highest point in the state, is in the Cascades. It stands 14,410 feet (4,392 meters) above sea level. Mount Saint Helens is also in this region. The Columbia River divides the state from north to south and forms much of the state's southern border. The Rocky Mountains cover northeastern Washington. The southeastern part of the state contains the Columbian Plateau.

PebbleGo Next Bonus! To watch a video on Mount Rainier National Park, go to www.pebblegonext.com and search keywords:

WA VIDEO

The San Juan islands of Puget Sound form an archipelago.

The Cascade Mountains carve through the middle of Washington.

Strait of Georgia

Strait of Juan de Fuca

Puget Sound

NORTH CASCADES NATIONAL PARK

Okanogan River

ROCKY MOUNTAINS

OLYMPIC MOUNTAINS

OLYMPIC NATIONAL PARK

PUGET SOUND LOWLANDS

CASCADE RANGE

Columbia River

COLUMBIA PLATEAU

PACIFIC OCEAN

Mount Rainier

MOUNT RAINIER NATIONAL PARK

Mount St. Helens

Hanford Reach

Snake River

Columbia River

Legend

▲ Highest Point

🏔 Mountain Range

▢ National Park

○ Point of Interest

〜 River

Scale

Miles
0 30 60 90

0 30 60 90 120
Kilometers

N W E S

WEATHER

Washington has cool winters. They average 33 degrees Fahrenheit (1 degree Celsius). Summers are mild. They average 64°F (18°C). Western Washington can be rainy and wet.

Average High and Low Temperatures (Seattle, WA)

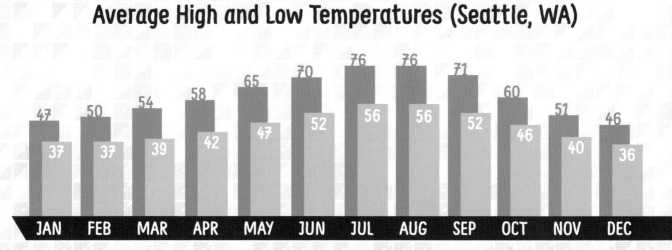

	JAN	FEB	MAR	APR	MAY	JUN	JUL	AUG	SEP	OCT	NOV	DEC
High	47	50	54	58	65	70	76	76	71	60	51	46
Low	37	37	39	42	47	52	56	56	52	46	40	36

LANDMARKS

Space Needle

The 605-foot-(184-meter-) tall Space Needle was built for the 1962 World's Fair. It has an observation deck and a rotating restaurant for people to enjoy views of the city, the water, and Mount Rainier.

Olympic National Park

Sometimes called three parks in one, Olympic National Park has tons of variety. Pacific coastlines, mountain views, and even a rain forest are all sites to enjoy in the park.

Mount Saint Helens National Volcanic Monument

Located about 100 miles (161 kilometers) from Seattle, Mount Saint Helens is an active volcano. In 1980, Mount Saint Helens had a large eruption that caused major damage to Washington's landscape. Visitor centers explain about volcanoes, eruptions, and how the land recovers after eruptions.

HISTORY AND GOVERNMENT

In 1775 the first European settlers to land at Washington were Bruno Heceta and Juan Francisco de la Bodega y Quadra.

American Indians once lived throughout Washington's wilderness. Explorers from several nations claimed parts of Washington during the 1700s. Russian fur traders from Alaska considered Washington their territory. Spanish explorers claimed land near the Quinault River in western Washington in 1775. British and American sailors also claimed some of Washington in the late 1700s. In 1803, the U.S. government bought much of the western United States from France. The sale was called the Louisiana Purchase. In 1846, the United States and Great Britain agreed on a boundary between their lands. The U.S. Congress created Washington Territory in 1853. Washington became the 42nd state in 1889.

Washington's state government is divided into legislative, executive, and judicial branches. The lawmaking legislature has two houses. They are the 49-member Senate and the 98-member House of Representatives. The governor leads the executive branch. The judicial branch is made up of judges and their courts.

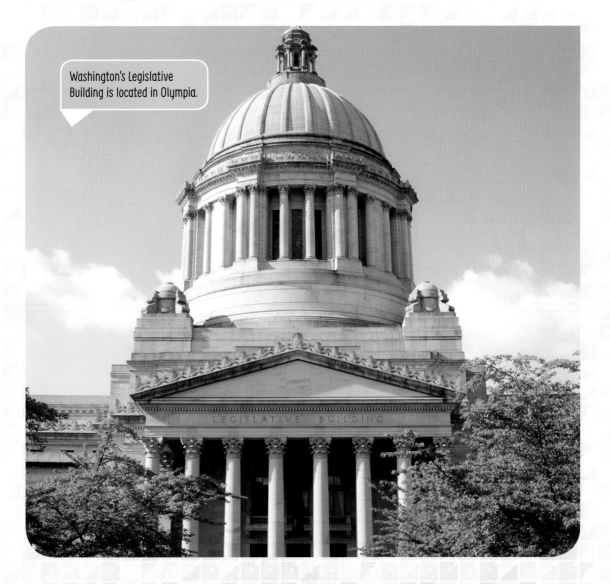

Washington's Legislative Building is located in Olympia.

INDUSTRY

Washington's economy relies on many industries. Tourism attracts boaters, hikers, skiers, and nature lovers.

Manufacturing is also important. Aerospace companies produce airplanes, rocket parts, and space equipment. Microsoft Corporation develops computer software. Washington workers build ships and make computers, electronics, and food products. The state's trees are used to make lumber, paper, and other wood products. Puget Sound and the Pacific Ocean provide fishing opportunities.

Manufacturing equipment for airplanes and rockets is an important industry in Washington.

Washington farmers grow more apples than any other state. Many farmers grow grains such as wheat and hops. The state is a leading producer of spearmint oil, lentils, and dry peas. It ranks second to Idaho in growing potatoes. Washington is also one of the world's main producers of flower bulbs.

Livestock also plays a role in the economy. Milk and beef are the most important livestock products in Washington. Farmers in the southeastern part of the state raise sheep.

Washington is home to many of the country's largest flower farms.

POPULATION

More than 70 percent of Washingtonians are white. Most of these people have European backgrounds. But the state has diversity as well. About 7 percent of the population is Asian. About 11 percent is Hispanic. A small population of African-Americans lives in Washington. The state is also home to Native Alaskan and American Indian people. Washington has more than 20 Indian reservations. The Yakama, Lummi, Quinault, Spokane, and Makah are some of the Indian groups living in Washington.

Population by Ethnicity

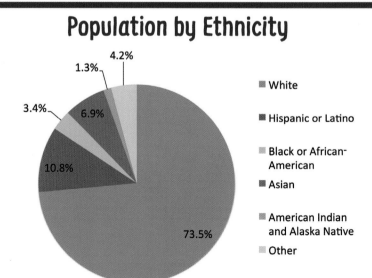

- White
- Hispanic or Latino
- Black or African-American
- Asian
- American Indian and Alaska Native
- Other

4.2%
1.3%
3.4%
6.9%
10.8%
73.5%

Source: U.S. Census Bureau.

People of all different backgrounds call the "Evergreen State" home.

FAMOUS PEOPLE

John Jacob Astor (1763–1848) owned the fur company that established Fort Okanogan, Washington's first permanent settlement, in 1811.

Sealth (1786–1866) was the chief of several American Indian tribes in the Puget Sound area. Seattle is named for him.

Bill Gates (1955–) is the founder of Microsoft, a computer software company. Gates is from Seattle and is one of the richest people in the world. The Microsoft headquarters is in Redmond.

Kasey Kahne (1980–) is a famous NASCAR stock car driver. He was born in Enumclaw.

Apolo Anton Ohno (1982–) is a retired U.S. Olympic speed skater. He has won more medals than any other U.S. winter Olympian. He was born in Federal Way.

Drew Bledsoe (1972–) played quarterback in the National Football League (NFL) for 14 years. He played for the New England Patriots, the Buffalo Bills, and the Dallas Cowboys. He was born in Ellensburg.

STATE SYMBOLS

Tree

western hemlock

Flower

coast rhododendron

Bird

willow goldfinch

Fruit

apple

PebbleGo Next Bonus! To make a dessert using the state fruit, go to www.pebblegonext.com and search keywords:

WA RECIPE

Marine Animal

orca

Vegetable

Walla Walla sweet onion

Amphibian

Pacific chorus frog

Grass

bluebunch wheatgrass

Fossil

Columbian mammoth

Insect

green darner dragonfly

21

FAST FACTS

STATEHOOD
1889

CAPITAL ☆
Olympia

LARGEST CITY •
Seattle

SIZE
66,456 square miles (172,120 square kilometers) land area
(2010 U.S. Census Bureau)

POPULATION
6,971,406 (2013 U.S. Census estimate)

STATE NICKNAME
Evergreen State

STATE MOTTO
"Al-ki," an American Indian word that means "by and by"

STATE SEAL

The state seal shows a portrait of the first president, George Washington. The state was named after him. At the bottom is 1889, the year Washington became a state.

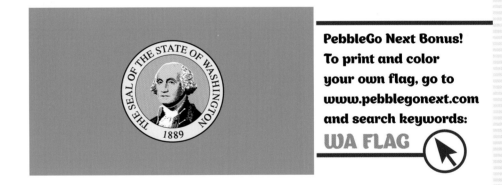

PebbleGo Next Bonus! To print and color your own flag, go to www.pebblegonext.com and search keywords:

WA FLAG

STATE FLAG

Washington adopted its state flag in 1923. The green background stands for Washington's evergreen forests. The state seal is in the center of the flag. The seal has a portrait of George Washington and the date 1889, for the year Washington became a state.

MINING PRODUCTS

gold, crushed stone, sand and gravel

MANUFACTURED GOODS

transportation equipment, petroleum and coal products, food products, computer and electronic equipment

FARM PRODUCTS

apples, wheat, grain, potatoes

PROFESSIONAL SPORTS TEAMS

Seattle Seahawks (NFL)
Seattle Mariners (MLB)
Seattle Sounders (MLS)
Seattle Storm (WNBA)

PebbleGo Next Bonus! To print a copy of the state song, go to www.pebblegonext.com and search keywords:

WA SONG

WASHINGTON TIMELINE

 **1620** The Pilgrims establish a colony in the New World in present-day Massachusetts.

 **1775** Bruno Heceta and Juan Francisco de la Bodega y Quadra become the first known Europeans to land on Washington soil.

 **1783** The American colonies win independence from Great Britain in the Revolutionary War (1775–1783).

 1792 Captain George Vancouver explores the Pacific Northwest.

1811
Fort Okanogan, the first United States settlement in Washington, is built.

 **1847**
Cayuse Indians kill the missionaries at the Whitman Mission near Walla Walla.

 **1853**
The U.S. Congress creates Washington Territory.

 **1861–1865**
The Union and the Confederacy fight the Civil War.

1889   Washington becomes the 42nd state on November 11.

1914–1918   World War I is fought; the United States enters the war in 1917.

1939–1945   World War II is fought; the United States enters the war in 1941.

1942   Grand Coulee Dam begins operation.

1962   The World's Fair is held in Seattle.

1980

Mount Saint Helens erupts on May 18. It destroys about 1,300 feet (400 m) of the volcano and kills 57 people.

1996

Gary Locke is elected governor of Washington, becoming the first Chinese-American governor in the nation.

2001

A strong earthquake shakes the Seattle area in February, causing more than $200 million in damage.

2007

The Washington State Legislature passes a bill establishing the Washington State Poet Laureate. This writer will compose poems for special occasions and find poems by other writers that Washingtonians might enjoy.

2014

On February 5 fans pack downtown Seattle for a victory parade celebrating the Seattle Seahawks' first-ever Super Bowl win. The parade turnout is the biggest gathering in Seattle's history with an estimated 450,000 people.

2014

On March 22, a massive landslide kills 41 people in the small northwestern towns of Darrington and Oso.

2015

Washington is one of the most productive growing regions in the world. As of April, the state ranks first in the nation in producing apples, grapes, sweet cherries, pears, and red raspberries. Washington has almost 40,000 farms growing over 300 specialty crops, which help fuel a diverse agricultural economy.

Glossary

archipelago *(ar-kuh-PE-luh-goh)*—a group of small islands

boundary *(BOUN-duh-ree)*—a border that separates one area from another

diversity *(di-VUR-suh-tee)*—the condition of being varied

economy *(i-KAH-nuh-mee)*—the ways in which a state handles its money and resources

eruption *(i-RUHP-shuhn)*—the action of throwing out rock, hot ash, and lava from a volcano with great force

executive *(ig-ZE-kyuh-tiv)*—the branch of government that makes sure laws are followed

industry *(IN-duh-stree)*—a business which produces a product or provides a service

legislature *(LEJ-iss-lay-chur)*—a group of elected officials who have the power to make or change laws for a country or state

lentil *(LEN-tuhl)*—the flat, round seed of a plant related to beans and peas

petroleum *(puh-TROH-lee-uhm)*—an oily liquid found below the earth's surface used to make gasoline, heating oil, and many other products

plateau *(pla-TOH)*—an area of high, flat land

region *(REE-juhn)*—a large area

Read More

Ganeri, Anita. *United States of America: A Benjamin Blog and His Inquisitive Dog Guide.* Country Guides. Chicago: Heinemann Raintree, 2015.

Kleinmartin, Hex. *Washington.* It's My State! New York: Cavendish Square Publishing, 2015.

Meinking, Mary. *What's Great About Washington?* Our Great States. Minneapolis: Lerner Publications, 2015.

Internet Sites

FactHound offers a safe, fun way to find Internet sites related to this book. All of the sites on FactHound have been researched by our staff.

Here's all you do:

Visit *www.facthound.com*

Type in this code: 9781515704355

 Check out projects, games and lots more at
www.capstonekids.com

Critical Thinking Using the Common Core

1. How does being by an ocean affect Washington's climate? (Integration of Knowledge and Ideas)

2. The Seattle Space Needle was created to be an attraction in honor of the 1962 World's Fair. It is now a landmark of the state. What are some landmarks in other cities you can think of? (Integration of Knowledge and Ideas)

3. There are many different industries that support Washington's economy. What are they? (Key Ideas and Details)

Index